Contents

Welcome to Id

Salaam Alaikum – peace be upon you. Welcome to the holy month of **Ramadan**, and to Id-ul-Fitr (or Id), the biggest festival in the Islamic year.

People send greetings cards to their friends and family at Id.

We Love ID-UL-FITR

Saviour Pirotta

Editor: Kirsty Hamilton
Senior Design Manager: Rosamund Saunders
Designer: Elaine Wilkinson

Published in Great Britain in 2006 by Wayland,
an imprint of Hachette Children's Books

Reprinted in 2007 and 2008

This paperback edition published in 2010 by Wayland,
a division of Hachette Children's Books.

British Library Cataloguing in Publication Data
Pirotta, Saviour
We love Id-ul-Fitr
1.Title
394.2'657

ISBN 9780750262071
Printed in China

Wayland
338 Euston Road, London NW1 3BH

Wayland is a division of Hachette Children's Books,
an Hachette UK Company.
www.hachette.co.uk

The publishers would like to thank the following for
allowing us to reproduce their pictures in this book:

Wayland Picture Library: 12 / Alamy: 4, 19,
ArkReligion.com; 5, Tina Manley; title page, 9, 11, Sally and
Richard Greenhill; 13, 17, World Religions Photo Library /
Corbis: 6, Thomas Hartwell; 10, Mian Khursheed; 14,
Reuters / World Religions Photo Library: 7, 8, 18, 20, 21,
22, Christine Osborne; 15, 23, cover, Paul Gapper; 16.
Richard Bell;

Ramadan is the month when the angel Jibril started giving the **Prophet** Muhammad ﷺ the words of **Allah**, the One God. These were written in the **Qur'an**, Islam's holy book. Muslims celebrate Ramadan to remember this very special month.

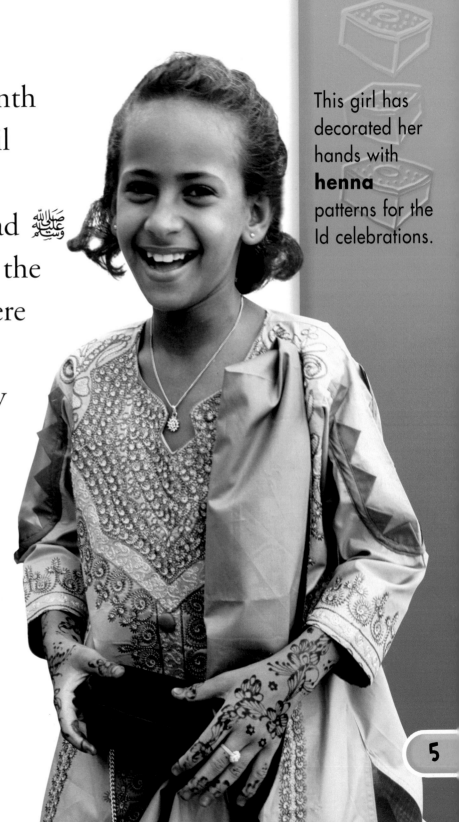

This girl has decorated her hands with **henna** patterns for the Id celebrations.

5

Fasting in Ramadan

During Ramadan, Muslims try to grow closer to Allah by reading the Qur'an and praying. They are careful not to say anything bad about anyone, or to listen to gossip about other people.

Muslim children go to school as usual at Ramadan.

Grown up Muslims and older children also **fast** between sunrise and sunset. That means they have no food or drink, not even water.

In the month of Ramadan, extra prayers are said throughout the day.

Beginning the fast

Everyone wakes up before dawn and families eat a meal called **Suhur**. The food varies from country to country.

At dawn, people are called to prayer at the **mosque** and the fasting begins.

Families read a special prayer from the Qur'an as they begin their fast.

In Egypt, many people have a simple breakfast of bread, yoghurt, cheese and tea. Suhur must be finished before sunrise.

Breaking the fast

This man in Pakistan is making Feni from sweet flour, to sell at the end of the daily fast.

When the sun goes down, Muslims break their fast and eat. Many choose a handful of dates and some water. That's how the Prophet Muhammad ﷺ broke his fast.

10

Later in the evening they have a bigger meal called **Ifthar**. They may invite friends to share it. Ifthar meals are delicious. In many countries people cook special Ramadan dishes.

11

The holiest night

Towards the end of Ramadan comes a very special night called the Night of Power, or Laylat-ul-Qadr. Muslims consider it the holiest night of the year. They believe it's when the angel Jibril started revealing the Qur'an to the Prophet ﷺ.

Some Muslims spend the last ten days of Ramadan at the mosque.

Many Muslims spend all night praying
and reading the Qur'an at the mosque.

The Qur'an
is believed to
show God's
own words.
This copy has
been carefully
decorated.

A new moon, a new celebration

Fasting ends on the last day of Ramadan. The first day of the next month, Shawwal, sees the celebration of Id-ul-Fitr. It starts when the new moon appears in the sky.

When the moon appears in this crescent shape it is known as a new moon.

14

People wear brand new clothes for Id. They go to the mosque where everybody greets each other with the words 'Id Mubarak', 'Blessed Id', 'Happy Id'.

These Muslims in India make sure they look their best for Id.

In the mosque

At the mosque there is a special Id prayer. Everyone says it together. Then their leader, the **Imam**, prays for all Muslims around the world. Everyone hugs friends and relatives.

Mosques like this one in Kuwait are lit up for Id.

Id is a time for thinking of others. Before the Id prayer starts, everyone gives some money for the poor.

The gifts of money and food given at Id are known as **zakat**.

DID YOU KNOW?

The special 'night prayer' that is recited at the mosque is called the Taraweeh.

Id mubarak

Id is mostly a family celebration. Many people decorate their homes with stars and moons. Some fill it with flowers.

In many countries there are street festivals with music and dancing.

This family have dressed in their best clothes for an Id festival in Malaysia.

Everyone sends Id cards and visits friends and relatives. Those who have argued during the year make up and shake hands.

DID YOU KNOW?

Children receive presents, new clothes and sometimes gifts of money too.

Treats at Id

These children in Morocco are buying delicious sweets at the Id market.

All over the world, Muslims have special food to celebrate Id. In Iraq, they have roast lamb, while in Egypt they prefer fish.

After fasting at Ramadan, Muslims look forward to special treats at Id. Iraqis and Palestinians make special pastry cases filled with chopped dates. In Indonesia they have a rich cake with vanilla and spices.

These special starters have been laid out for a wonderful Id feast.

21

End of Id

The Id feast is the first time in a month that many have eaten during the day. Afterwards, they thank Allah for helping them keep the fast through Ramadan.

These Muslims in Tanzania are celebrating Id with music and singing.

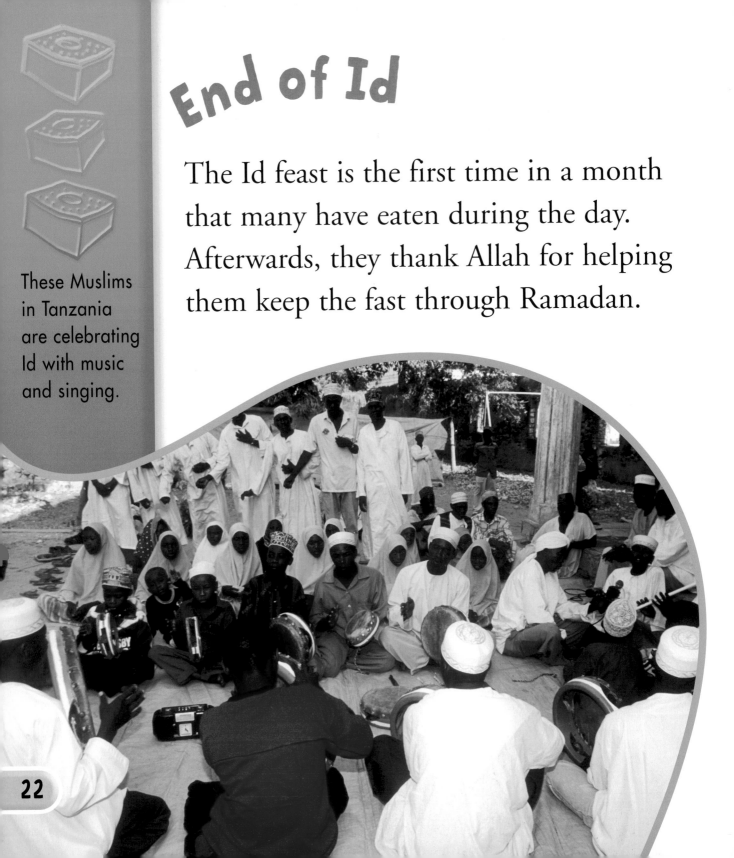

It has made them think about people less lucky than themselves. It has also made them feel close to all other Muslims around the world.

Friends and relatives hug and greet each other at Id.

Index and glossary

Allah the Muslim name for God

fast to go without food or drink

henna a red dye used to decorate skin and colour hair

Ifthar the evening meal that Muslims have during Ramadan

Imam a Muslim religious leader

Mosque the building where Muslims meet for worship

Prophet someone who gives people messages from God

Qu'ran the Holy Book of Islam

Ramadan the month in the Islamic year when people fast

Suhur the meal eaten before sunrise during Ramadan

Zakat special gifts of money or food that are given to the poor